ENDANGERED AND THREATENED ANIMALS

THE BALD EAGLE

A MyReportLinks.com Book

Cheryl L. DeFries

MyReportLinks.com Books
an imprint of
Enslow Publishers, Inc. E
Box 398, 40 Industrial Road
Berkeley Heights, NJ 07922
USA

199 83/5

To my beloved husband, Dave, and our three children:
Danielle, David, and Denise. Love Eternally, Mom

MyReportLinks.com Books, an imprint of Enslow Publishers, Inc. MyReportLinks is
a trademark of Enslow Publishers, Inc.

Library of Congress Cataloging-in-Publication Data

DeFries, Cheryl L.
  The bald eagle / Cheryl L. DeFries.
      p. cm. — (Endangered and threatened animals)
Summary: Examines the habitat and physical characteristics of the bald
eagle and its threatened status. Includes Internet links to Web sites
related to bald eagles. Includes bibliographical references (p.   ).
  ISBN 0-7660-5057-2
  1. Bald eagle—Juvenile literature. 2. Endangered species—Juvenile
literature. [1. Bald eagle. 2. Eagles. 3. Endangered species.] I.
Title. II. Series.
  QL696.F32 D43 2003
  598.9'43—dc21

                                    2002151797

Printed in the United States of America

10 9 8 7 6 5 4 3 2 1

To Our Readers:
Through the purchase of this book, you and your library gain access to the Report Links that specifically back
up this book.
The Publisher will provide access to the Report Links that back up this book and will keep these Report Links
up to date on **www.myreportlinks.com** for three years from the book's first publication date.
We have done our best to make sure all Internet addresses in this book were active and appropriate when we
went to press. However, the author and the Publisher have no control over, and assume no liability for, the
material available on those Internet sites or on other Web sites they may link to.
The usage of the MyReportLinks.com Books Web site is subject to the terms and conditions stated on the
Usage Policy Statement on **www.myreportlinks.com**.
In the future, a password may be required to access the Report Links that back up this book. The password
is found on the bottom of page 4 of this book.
Any comments or suggestions can be sent by e-mail to comments@myreportlinks.com or to the address on
the back cover.

Photo Credits: American Eagle Foundation, pp. 32, 38; © Corel Corporation, pp. 1, 3, 10, 11, 13,
14, 17, 26, 28, 30, 35, 36, 43; © Gary Bromberger/Midwest Eagles 2000, p. 41; © 1998–2003
GreatSeal.com, p. 34; © 1999–2003 Animals of the Rainforest/Michael Myers, p. 22; © 1996
American Museum of Natural History, p. 16; © 1996–2002 baldeagleinfo.com, pp. 20, 24; © 2001
GetOutdoors.com, p. 37; John Bavaro, p. 18; MyReportLinks.com Books, p. 4; U.S. Fish and Wildlife
Service, p. 44.

Cover Photo: © Corel Corporation

Contents

About MyReportLinks.com Books

MyReportLinks.com Books
Great Books, Great Links, Great for Research!

MyReportLinks.com Books present the information you need to learn about your report subject. In addition, they show you where to go on the Internet for more information. The pre-evaluated Report Links that back up this book are kept up to date on **www.myreportlinks.com**. With the purchase of a MyReportLinks.com Books title, you and your library gain access to the Report Links that specifically back up that book. The Report Links save hours of research time and link to dozens—even hundreds—of Web sites, source documents, and photos related to your report topic.

Please see "To Our Readers" on the Copyright page for important information about this book, the MyReportLinks.com Books Web site, and the Report Links that back up this book.

Access:

The Publisher will provide access to the Report Links that back up this book and will try to keep these Report Links up to date on our Web site for three years from the book's first publication date. Please enter **EBE6624** if asked for a password.

Report Links

The Internet sites described below can be accessed at
http://www.myreportlinks.com

▶ **American Bald Eagle Information**   *EDITOR'S CHOICE

The American Bald Eagle Information Web site provides
comprehensive information about the bald eagle. Here you will learn
about the bird's physical attributes, its history, feeding habits,
and much more.

Link to this Internet site from http://www.myreportlinks.com

▶ **National Wildlife Federation**   *EDITOR'S CHOICE

The National Wildlife Federation Web site provides a brief overview of
the bald eagle. There are links to information about the history of the
bald eagle, scientific facts, video clips, and a section that tells people
how they can help bald eagles.

Link to this Internet site from http://www.myreportlinks.com

▶ **The American Museum of Natural History**   *EDITOR'S CHOICE

Read how loss of habitat, human encroachment, and a decline in prey
have contributed to near extinction of the bald eagle. Learn how this
raptor was brought back from the brink of total loss.

Link to this Internet site from http://www.myreportlinks.com

▶ **Kids' Planet**   *EDITOR'S CHOICE

Kids' Planet offers fact sheets on over fifty species, including the bald
eagle. You can also explore ways to protect the environment and how to
contribute to the cause.

Link to this Internet site from http://www.myreportlinks.com

▶ **National Parks Conservation Association**   *EDITOR'S CHOICE

The National Parks Conservation Association presents fascinating facts
and images of wildlife. Learn about wildlife protection, take a cyber
safari, and see the biodiversity of America's national parks and wildlife.

Link to this Internet site from http://www.myreportlinks.com

▶ **Bald Eagle**   *EDITOR'S CHOICE

This Web site includes information about the anatomy of the bald eagle,
its habitat range, background information, and conservation efforts.
You will also find details about the bald eagle's diet and migration.

Link to this Internet site from http://www.myreportlinks.com

Report Links

The Internet sites described below can be accessed at
http://www.myreportlinks.com

American Bald Eagle Foundation
This is an educational foundation dedicated to the protection and preservation of the bald eagle. Learn about the year-round home for bald eagles in Alaska.

Link to this Internet site from http://www.myreportlinks.com

American Eagle Foundation
This foundation offers a lot of information about the bald eagle. See the "Great Eagle Seal," and learn what it means. You will also find extensive information about other North American birds of prey.

Link to this Internet site from http://www.myreportlinks.com

Animals of the Rainforest: Bald Eagle
The bald eagle belongs to the animal kingdom, but do you know what phylum and class it belongs to? You will after you read these interesting and educational facts. Photos of the bald eagle are included.

Link to this Internet site from http://www.myreportlinks.com

Bagheera: Spotlight
At this Web site you will find an overview of the bald eagle and other endangered species. You will also find information about the Endangered Species Act.

Link to this Internet site from http://www.myreportlinks.com

The Birds of Prey Foundation
Learn how to care for and treat injured birds. Learn about hawks and other raptors, including the eagle. View photos from the intensive care unit for injured birds of prey. Learn how the birds are cared for and then released back into the wild.

Link to this Internet site from http://www.myreportlinks.com

Canadian Wildlife Service Hinterland's Who's Who
The Canadian Wildlife Service offers information about the bald eagle and other birds of prey. View a map that shows the distribution of the bald eagle during wintering and breeding times.

Link to this Internet site from http://www.myreportlinks.com

Report Links

The Internet sites described below can be accessed at
http://www.myreportlinks.com

▶ The Carolina Raptor Center

Research, rehabilitation, and education about raptors are just some of the topics offered by the Carolina Raptor Center. Learn about migration, and view images from webcams that include the bald eagle.

Link to this Internet site from http://www.myreportlinks.com

▶ The Eagle Institute

Did you know that eagles mate for life? Find this and other information about the bald eagle, its habitat, and migration at the Eagle Institute. You will also find photos and maps.

Link to this Internet site from http://www.myreportlinks.com

▶ Endangered Species

This Web site offers an abundance of information about endangered species. Here you will find definitions, endangered species lists, international organizations, and much more.

Link to this Internet site from http://www.myreportlinks.com

▶ Endangered Species Coalition

At this Web site you will learn about the efforts of the Endangered Species Coalition. You will also find hot topics related to endangered species.

Link to this Internet site from http://www.myreportlinks.com

▶ GreatSeal.com: Great Seal of the United States

Read quotes from America's founding fathers about the symbolism of the bald eagle. You can also view the Great Seal of the United States and learn what the parts of the seal stand for. Original artwork is included.

Link to this Internet site from http://www.myreportlinks.com

▶ Marco Island's Bald Eagle

View beautiful photos as well as interesting information and statistics about the bald eagle. You can also read about the progress in the fight for preservation.

Link to this Internet site from http://www.myreportlinks.com

Report Links

The Internet sites described below can be accessed at
http://www.myreportlinks.com

MidWestEagles.com
How good is the eyesight of an eagle? The answer to this and other interesting facts are waiting behind each photo of the bald eagle.

Link to this Internet site from http://www.myreportlinks.com

National Audubon Society
From the National Audubon Society comes information about the birding world. Up-to-the-minute news, photos and information about the bald eagle, as well as birds from all over the world, are presented.

Link to this Internet site from http://www.myreportlinks.com

Nebraska Wildlife: The Bald Eagle
Learn about "Nebraska's Winter Visitors" and how the bald eagle is making a comeback in this area of the United States. View a map of wintering distribution in Nebraska, and read about the bald eagle's habits, habitat, and food.

Link to this Internet site from http://www.myreportlinks.com

Northern Prairie Wildlife Research Center: The Bald Eagle in Oklahoma
Oklahoma is an important wintering area for the bald eagle. Learn more about this, the eagle's decline, and nesting eagles. Be sure to check out the "What you should know" section to learn about how to report violations.

Link to this Internet site from http://www.myreportlinks.com

Northeast Utilities
View a picture gallery showing bald eagles in action taken from a working 'eaglecam.' You can also learn about the Eagle Festival in Connecticut and interesting facts about the bald eagle.

Link to this Internet site from http://www.myreportlinks.com

The Raptor Center
Read how this international medical facility for birds of prey works to preserve biological diversity among raptors and other avian species. There is a "Jump To" section where you can select which raptor you wish to learn about.

Link to this Internet site from http://www.myreportlinks.com

Any comments? Contact us: **comments@myreportlinks.com**

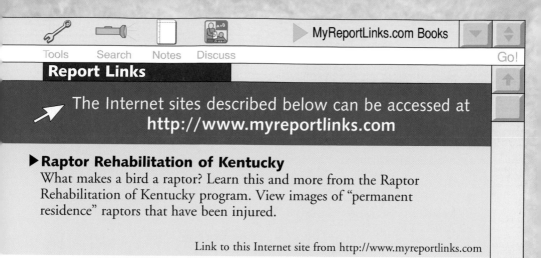

Report Links

The Internet sites described below can be accessed at
http://www.myreportlinks.com

▶ **Raptor Rehabilitation of Kentucky**
What makes a bird a raptor? Learn this and more from the Raptor
Rehabilitation of Kentucky program. View images of "permanent
residence" raptors that have been injured.

Link to this Internet site from http://www.myreportlinks.com

▶ **SeaWorld Busch Gardens: Birds of Prey**
Many facts are presented about the bald eagle, including classification,
habitat, senses, and behavior. The Anatomy and Physiology sections
provide interesting information about birds of prey.

Link to this Internet site from http://www.myreportlinks.com

▶ **South Dakota Department of Agriculture:**
Bald Eagle Awareness Days
Where can you go to see bald eagles in South Dakota? Learn this, and
other interesting facts about both the bald and golden eagles. Safe and
responsible eagle-watching information is also provided.

Link to this Internet site from http://www.myreportlinks.com

▶ **U.S. Fish & Wildlife Service:**
Endangered Species Program
At the U.S. Fish & Wildlife Service Web site, you can learn about the
bald eagle and other endangered species.

Link to this Internet site from http://www.myreportlinks.com

▶ **Washington Department of Fish and Wildlife**
The Washington Department of Fish and Wildlife presents live cameras
covering the day-to-day activities of the bald eagle and other wildlife.
Journal entries about nesting bald eagles in Australia are also included.

Link to this Internet site from http://www.myreportlinks.com

▶ **World Wildlife Fund: Endangered Species**
At this Web site you can learn about endangered species, read recent
news about endangered and threatened species, and ways that you can
help protect the environment.

Link to this Internet site from http://www.myreportlinks.com

Bald Eagle Facts

▶ **Class**

Aves

▶ **Family**

Accipitridae

▶ **Genus**

Haliaeetus

▶ **Species**

leucocephalus

▶ **Average Length**

32 inches
(81.28 centimeters)

▶ **Average Weight**

9 pounds
(4.08 kilograms)

▶ **Life Span**

Between 15 and 40 years

▶ **Range**

The Continental United States and parts of Canada.

▶ **Status**

Listed as a threatened species by the U.S. Fish and Wildlife service, but proposed for delisting.

▶ **Color**

White heads, necks, and tails; yellow eyes and beaks; and dark brown bodies.

▶ **Diet**

Mainly fish

▶ **Gestation Period**

Eggs hatch in about thirty-five days

▶ **Threats to Survival**

Eating contaminated fish; flying into power lines; illegal shooting; starvation.

▶ **Voice**

The bald eagle's call sound is "kar, kar, kar."

The Bald Eagle

The bald eagle glides effortlessly in a slow, lazy circle in the sky. Its eight-foot wings seem to hold it suspended in the air. This giant, majestic bird can soar this way for hours, using natural wind currents and thermals. As it glides, its sharp, yellow eyes search the river below for food. Then, the eagle spots a fish near the surface, nearly a mile away. It swoops down toward the surface of the water at

▲ Bald eagles will prey on almost any animal that is easy to obtain—and within their four-pound lifting power. However, they mostly eat fish, and almost always nest by large bodies of water regardless of whether they are fresh-or saltwater.

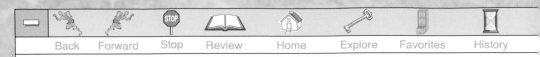
more than one hundred miles per hour. Its long, sharp talons are out in front to grab the fish and lift it from the water. With several strong flaps of its wings, the eagle climbs into the sky, the fish locked firmly in its claws.

For centuries, American Indians and bald eagles lived in harmony. The bird represented strength to American Indians. Eagle feathers were used in ceremonies and proudly displayed in headdresses. Human and bird shared what nature provided, and bald eagles had nothing to fear from the native peoples. Many tribes considered the majestic bird sacred. Bald eagles ruled the skies.

That all changed after 1621, when European settlers arrived in North America. The immigrants shared the land with an estimated 500,000 bald eagles. The birds nested in three main places: the tops of very tall trees, along the coastline, and deep in the forest. They built their nests and raised their young in undisturbed surroundings. As more and more settlers arrived, pioneers cleared the wilderness to make room for towns and farms. The logs cut from the forests became fuel and lumber for the settlers. Rivers, lakes, and streams containing the food for the bald eagles also provided food for settlers. Human and bird competed for food, but the bald eagle was no match against the bullet from a settler's gun. The bald eagle's enemy became the encroaching settler. In order to survive, bald eagles had to find new homes and nesting areas. Even so, the bald eagle population was decreasing sharply by the late 1800s.

Then, in the late twentieth century, humans accidentally dealt another blow to the dwindling bald eagle population. People began using DDT, a strong and effective pesticide, to kill pests that threatened farm crops. The chemical leaked into streams and other waterways, contaminating the water. This poisoned the fish that were

▲ Toxic chemicals, such as DDT, were a major contributor to the decline in the number of bald eagles.

the main source of food for eagles. It took decades before people discovered that DDT was wiping out both insects and bald eagles. By the early 1960s, there were fewer than 450 nesting pairs in the United States. The bald eagle almost became extinct, meaning there are no living members of a species left. The questions often asked are: how could this happen, and what have people done to help the bald eagle?

Chapter 2

Profile of a Bald Eagle

The bald eagle is a raptor, or a bird of prey, because it hunts, kills, and eats other birds and mammals. Hawks, vultures, and falcons, for example, are also raptors. Bald eagles will kill prey only when they are hungry, or to feed their young. Eagles belong to the fish and sea eagle group that first appeared on earth about 25 million years ago.

The average life span of a bald eagle in the wild is about fifteen to twenty years, although some may live to be thirty years old. In captivity, where humans provide food and security, eagles can live up to forty years.

▲ *At times, bald eagles must dive into the water to catch their prey. They use their strong wings to help them swim—an activity they are very good at.*

▷ Habitats

Bald eagles usually build their nests far away from people. However, they often hunt and roost near humans during daylight hours. The birds seek out wooded areas to build their nests near coastlines, lakes, rivers, and marshes where fish are plentiful. Occasionally, an eagle will build its nest on top of a cliff rather than in tall trees. However, it will only nest in those areas that provide enough food and nesting area to support the adult eagles and its young.

▷ Range

The bald eagle is the only eagle to live entirely in North America. It can be found in every state, except Hawaii. Bald eagles also nest in northern Mexico and western Canada. On the other hand, they are not usually found in the desert regions of North America. In contrast, golden eagles, the other type of eagle commonly found throughout the Western Hemisphere, can be spotted in northern Africa, Asia, and Europe as well.

▷ Migration

Bald eagles do not migrate from one place to another because of cold weather. They migrate to find food. If there is enough food, the eagles will stay in their nesting area year-round. When winter arrives in the north and freezes the waterways, bald eagles will migrate south or to the coastline in search of food.

Bald eagles rely on thermals and updrafts to migrate. Thermals are layers of warm air just above the earth's surface caused by long periods of sunny skies. Thermals help the eagles to glide, which conserves energy on their long migration route. Soaring high on a strong thermal, they

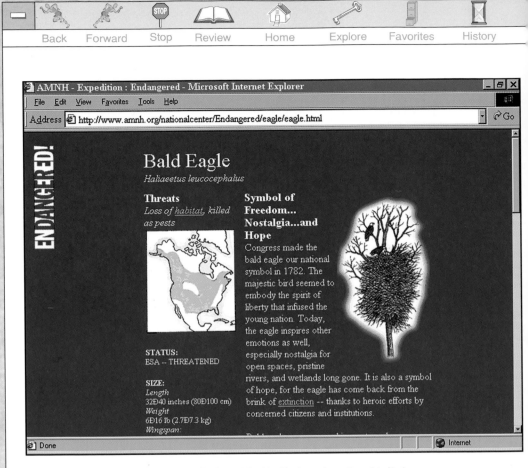

ENDANGERED!

Bald Eagle
Haliaeetus leucocephalus

Threats
Loss of habitat, killed as pests

STATUS:
ESA -- THREATENED

SIZE:
Length
32Ð40 inches (80Ð100 cm)
Weight
6Ð16 lb (2.7Ð7.3 kg)
Wingspan:

Symbol of Freedom... Nostalgia...and Hope
Congress made the bald eagle our national symbol in 1782. The majestic bird seemed to embody the spirit of liberty that infused the young nation. Today, the eagle inspires other emotions as well, especially nostalgia for open spaces, pristine rivers, and wetlands long gone. It is also a symbol of hope, for the eagle has come back from the brink of extinction -- thanks to heroic efforts by concerned citizens and institutions.

▲ Bald eagles are only found in North America. One bird's home range will span anywhere from 1,700 to 10,000 acres depending upon the availability of food.

glide or circle downward until they find another thermal. This process is repeated often. An updraft occurs when wind strikes something tall, such as a mountain. The wind deflects off the mountain and is pushed upward. Eagles use these to help them soar hire.

Bald eagles migrate in groups, known as kettles, during the day.[1] They spread out about half a mile apart, forming a group, or stream, that can be twenty to thirty miles long. The kettle averages speeds of thirty miles per hour.

By the time winter arrives, bald eagles often have gathered in large numbers where fish and other foods are plentiful.

When spring arrives, they quickly migrate back to their nesting areas.

Young bald eagles usually migrate before their parents. Over their first few years, some fledglings cover a large area during migration. Why this happens is still a mystery.

▲ *Only about one in every eighteen attacks on prey are successful. Although they do not have to eat every day, quite a bit of energy is used in these attacks, forcing bald eagles to spend a lot of time resting.*

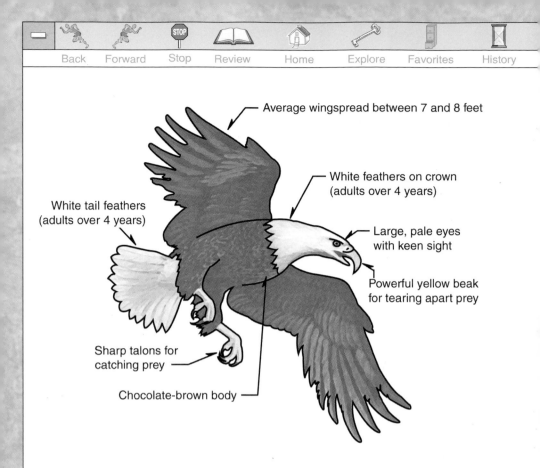

Average wingspread between 7 and 8 feet

White feathers on crown
(adults over 4 years)

White tail feathers
(adults over 4 years)

Large, pale eyes
with keen sight

Powerful yellow beak
for tearing apart prey

Sharp talons for
catching prey

Chocolate-brown body

▶ Types of Bald Eagles

There are two subspecies of the bald eagle: the northern bald eagle and the southern bald eagle. Northern bald eagles are a little larger and slightly heavier than southern bald eagles.

▶ Physical Description

Whether they are the northern or southern subspecies, bald eagles are larger than most North American raptors. Only the California condor is larger, while golden eagles are about the same size.

Male bald eagles are smaller than female bald eagles. Males measure about thirty-one to thirty-six inches from head to tail. They weigh between seven and ten pounds, and have a wingspan of about six feet, six inches. Females weigh up to fourteen pounds and have a wingspan of up to eight feet. Another difference between the male and female bald eagle is the size of their beaks. The female's beak is larger.

Adult bald eagles are easy to recognize. They have white feathers on their heads, throats, wing tips, and tails. The feathers on their trunks and legs are brown. Despite the name, the bald eagle is not really bald. The name came from the Old English word, *balde*, which means "white."

The skeleton of a bald eagle is very light—it weighs about half a pound (.23kg). As with all birds, the bald eagle's bones are filled with air pockets. This allows the bird to be light enough to fly. Braces, called *struts*, inside the bones make them very strong. Like all birds, the bald eagle is warm-blooded. Its normal body temperature is 102°F or 38.8°C.

About seven thousand feathers, known as *plumage*, cover bald eagles' bodies. Altogether, their feathers weigh about one pound (.45kg). Keratin, a protein found in human hair and fingernails makes their feathers, beaks, and talons strong.

The eagle has several different types of feathers. Those that cover the body and give it shape are called contour feathers. The feathers that help the bird fly are called flight feathers. Down feathers, which are small and fluffy, lie next to the eagle's skin under the contour feathers. The down protects the eagle from cold, heat, and rain by trapping air between overlapping feathers. In flight, the bald eagle uses its tail feathers to steer toward prey, change direction, dive, slow down, and land.

Bald eagles' legs, feet, and two-inch hooked beaks are bright yellow. The eagle's powerful beak is used to rip and

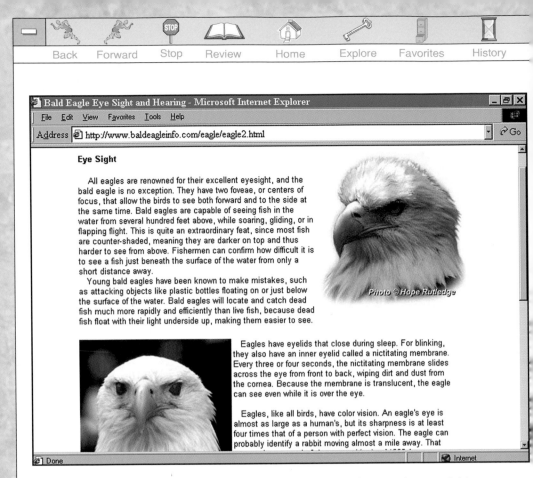

Eye Sight

All eagles are renowned for their excellent eyesight, and the bald eagle is no exception. They have two foveae, or centers of focus, that allow the birds to see both forward and to the side at the same time. Bald eagles are capable of seeing fish in the water from several hundred feet above, while soaring, gliding, or in flapping flight. This is quite an extraordinary feat, since most fish are counter-shaded, meaning they are darker on top and thus harder to see from above. Fishermen can confirm how difficult it is to see a fish just beneath the surface of the water from only a short distance away.

Young bald eagles have been known to make mistakes, such as attacking objects like plastic bottles floating on or just below the surface of the water. Bald eagles will locate and catch dead fish much more rapidly and efficiently than live fish, because dead fish float with their light underside up, making them easier to see.

Eagles have eyelids that close during sleep. For blinking, they also have an inner eyelid called a nictitating membrane. Every three or four seconds, the nictitating membrane slides across the eye from front to back, wiping dirt and dust from the cornea. Because the membrane is translucent, the eagle can see even while it is over the eye.

Eagles, like all birds, have color vision. An eagle's eye is almost as large as a human's, but its sharpness is at least four times that of a person with perfect vision. The eagle can probably identify a rabbit moving almost a mile away. That

Photo © Hope Rutledge

▲ Bald eagles rely on their excellent vision to catch prey. Their eyesight is four to six times better than a human's. This allows these birds to see any prey within three miles, even at heights of 1,000 feet.

tear apart its prey. However, the beak also delicately feeds and preens (cleans) its chicks.

Without their impressive speed and strength, bald eagles would not be the successful hunters we know them to be. Their powerful legs and feet give them great strength. Their legs have feathers halfway down to their feet. Yellow, scaly skin covers the lower part of their legs. They have four toes on each foot. Three toes are in the front and one toe is in the back. Each toe has a tough, four-inch (10.16 cm), knife-like, black, curved talon (claw). The bottom surface of their toes has tiny spicules (spikes) that help them grasp their prey. Eagles can lift a fish or animal that weighs around four pounds (1.81kg). They also use their talons for fighting and courtship.

Bald eagles have excellent vision. Their pale, yellow eyes have two centers of focus. This permits them to see forward and to the side at the same time. Their eye size is another advantage. Despite having small heads, bald eagles have eyes that are almost as large as human eyes. This is one reason the bald eagle can see four to eight times better than a human can. People see just three basic colors. Eagles see five. This allows them to more easily distinguish between colors helping them to pick out even well-camouflaged prey from a great distance. A bald eagle can spot a rabbit sitting on the ground more than a mile (1.6 km) away.

Bald eagles keep their eyes clean with a clear inner membrane, called the *nictitating membrane*. When they blink, the membrane glides across the eye and wipes the surface of the eye clean. Because the nictitating membrane is clear, the eagle can still see through it although it covers part of the eye. When the eagle sleeps, however, its eyelids close.

To communicate, the bald eagle has a squeaky voice that seems to cackle. Sometimes its voice sounds high-pitched and piercing, like a fingernail scraping across a chalkboard. A bald eagle may use this call to communicate with others, including its mate. The bald eagle also uses its loud calls to warn predators that have come too close to its nest.[4]

Nesting and Reproduction

Bald eagles mate only once a year, and it is for life. They will only take another mate only when their mate dies. Bald eagle courtship begins at different times for the two subspecies. Southern bald eagles' mating season runs from

▲ Bald eagles typically build their nests in trees near water. These nests are often five feet in diameter, but due to extended use over the years, they can grow to ten feet (3.05 m) in diameter, weighing almost two thousand pounds (907.19 kg).

late September to the end of November. In the north, mating takes place from January through April.

Their spectacular mating ritual takes place in the sky. The male and female chase and dive at each other. They lock their talons in midair, make death-defying loops, and tumble downward. Just before reaching the earth, they release their talons and soar skyward again. This aerial routine occurs many times. Mating itself does not occur in flight; they usually mate while perched on a tree branch.

The bald eagle's nest is called an *eyrie* or *aerie*. It is made of twigs and large sticks and is lined with pine needles, twigs, grass, soft moss, and feathers. Throughout the nesting season, bald eagles bring fresh green twigs to the nest. This keeps the nest in good condition and helps to secure a lasting bond between the mated pair of eagles. They build the nest to last, as mated eagles use the same nest year after year, often for a lifetime. The bald eagles will rebuild a new nest, often in the same area, only if their nest is destroyed. The nests themselves are huge. Bald eagles build larger nests than nearly all other birds in the world. A typical bald eagle nest is two feet (.61m) deep and five feet (1.52 m) wide in its early years. Older nests may reach ten feet (3.04 m) wide, and weigh almost two thousand pounds (907 kg). Bald eagles usually build their nests within one hundred miles (160.93 kg) of where they were born.

The shape and size of tree branches determine the shape of the bald eagle's nest. Sticks placed in the deep fork of a branch result in a cone-shaped nest. When the nest is built on the ground or on level branches, it is disk-shaped. Bowl-shaped nests occur where the tree branches are smaller and upright.

▷ Eggs

Females lay a clutch of eggs, no more than three, once a year. If the eggs are destroyed, the female may lay more eggs. The eggs are laid several days apart. Bald eagle eggs, ranging from dull white to creamy yellow in color, are about 3 inches (7.62 cm) long and 2 inches (5.08 cm) wide. Once the eggs are laid, both parents take turns sitting on them to keep them warm until they hatch. This is called incubation. In addition to incubation, the parent who stays with the eggs must protect them from squirrels, ravens, and gulls. These animals will eat bald eagle eggs. Occasionally, larger animals, such as raccoons, may also try to steal an egg from an undefended nest. Both male and female bald eagles fiercely protect their nesting and feeding areas, but if people approach these sites too closely, bald eagles may abandon their nest and eggs.

▶ Eaglets

The eaglet, also called a chick, hatches in about thirty-four days. The chick uses its "egg tooth" to break through the shell. The egg tooth forms on the end of what will be the beak of a chick. The chick may peck at its shell for a few hours or up to two days, before breaking out of it. Over the next few days, the other eaglets will also hatch.

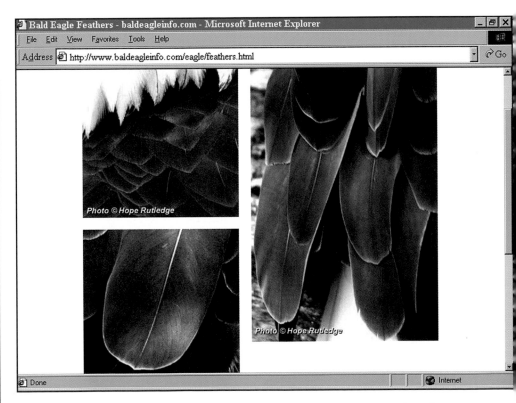

Bald eagles have over seven thousand feathers that protect them from the cold and rain.

Still, there are many hazards ahead for newborn chicks. Sometimes, the firstborn or the strongest eaglet kills its weaker siblings. The older eaglets often consume most of the food brought to the nest by the parents, leaving the smaller eaglets to starve. Young chicks are susceptible to disease, bad weather, and/or human interference. Only about half of all eaglets survive their first year.

Newly-hatched eaglets are usually about four inches (10.16 cm) tall and weight between three and four ounces (85.05 to 113.39 grams). They are born with fuzzy, gray down feathers. By four weeks, they have grown thicker. At about six weeks, they begin to grow their juvenile feathers.

By the time the eaglet is thirteen weeks old, drab, brown feathers with blotches of white appear on the underwings, belly, and back. Juvenile bald eagles are often confused with young golden eagles, because their coloring is similar. Juvenile bald eagles do not get their distinctive white head, neck, and tail feathers until they are mature at four or five years old.

Both parents brood (care) for the hungry new hatchlings. The eaglets eat almost as much as their parents. To keep up with the eaglets' appetites, one parent will hunt for food while the other protects the eaglets and keeps them warm. Occasionally, a young eaglet is taken from an unguarded nest by a great horned owl.

Between sixty-five and eighty-four days, the eaglets will begin to *fledge*. This means that they lose their loose down and develop feathers that can support flight. They are now called fledglings. The parents will continue to feed the chicks for four to six weeks while they teach them how to hunt. Once the fledglings learn how to hunt for themselves, they will no longer depend on their parents for food.

By this time, the young bald eagles have their risky first year behind them. Although the death rate for young bald eagles starts out greater than 50 percent, once they learn to hunt, they have an excellent chance of reaching adulthood.

▷ Hunting

These magnificent birds hunt only during the day, usually alone, but sometimes in pairs. Bald eagles do not always find food every day, and during lean times, they can go for one or more days without food. They can also store their food when it is plentiful. Eagles have a *crop*, or pouch, in

▲ Bald eagles are able to consume one pound of fish in approximately four minutes.

their throat, where they can store food. About 70 percent of the bald eagle's food is fish, which the eagle hunts for in both salt- and freshwater. They will also hunt small mammals such as rabbits, rodents, snakes, turtles, and waterfowl. Sometimes bald eagles feed on carrion (dead animals that have begun to decompose) that can be found on roads. This puts bald eagles in constant danger of being hit by motor vehicles.

Because they do not always hunt their food, bald eagles have been called pirates. They commonly steal food from ospreys and other birds by harassing them in flight until they drop their prey. The bald eagle can then catch the falling prey in midair with its talons. Bald eagle talons have a special locking mechanism. When the open talons hit the prey, they instantly close. The talons cannot open again until the eagle pushes down on a solid surface.

Bald eagles are skilled at swooping down and seizing fish near the surface of the water. When necessary, eagles will swim, using an overhead movement of the wings that looks like the butterfly stroke. This movement helps them get a heavy fish to shore.

If food is abundant, bald eagles can restrict their hunting grounds to a small area. If food is scarce, the eagle will cover a vast area, from 1,700 to 10,000 acres.

Because bald eagles also feed on dead animals, they are known as scavengers. This activity actually helps the environment by removing dead animals that could otherwise spread disease. Eagles also help by killing weaker, older, and slower animals. The strongest animals remain. In this way, bald eagles play an important role in keeping a healthy and well-balanced environment.

Chapter 3 ▶

A Threatened Species

Bald eagles have few natural enemies. Their greatest enemies are people. Four reasons are usually given for the decline of the bald eagle. They are: loss of habitat; loss of nesting trees; illegal shooting; and the chemical insecticide dichloro-diphenyl-trichloroethane, known more simply as DDT.[1]

Early settlers saw the bald eagle as a threat to their livestock. They claimed the birds killed and carried off their

▲ As a predator resting at the top of the food chain, bald eagles do not have many natural threats. Humans have become the bird's greatest enemy.

animals. Farmers, hunters, anglers, and ranchers trapped, poisoned, and shot the birds in large numbers. Sometimes bounties (rewards) were paid for killing bald eagles. By the time the bounties were removed in 1953, over one hundred thousand eagles had been killed.[2]

Human Carelessness

Other acts of recklessness took place as people moved into the bald eagle's habitat. Early settlers, modern farmers, and loggers cleared land the eagles used for nesting grounds. People competed with bald eagles for animals from the forest and fish from the waters. Feeding and nesting habitats of the bald eagle began to disappear.

The number of bald eagles was rapidly decreasing because of human carelessness. However, people were not finished with the bald eagle. We had unknowingly created another way to reduce the number of bald eagles to a level near extinction; we made DDT.

DDT

After World War II, a very powerful pesticide, called DDT, was sprayed on farm crops to kill insects. It was widely used, because one application of DDT could kill hundreds of insects. Rainwater washed the deadly chemical into lakes and streams, poisoning the bald eagle's food—fish, birds, and mammals.

When bald eagles ate the contaminated food, they also became poisoned by the DDT. The pesticide, stored in the bird's fat, reduced female production of calcium, which is needed for bone growth and for eggshell strength. When the poisoned female bald eagle laid eggs, the shells were thin and weak. The weight of the parents would often crush many of the eggs during incubation.

▲ *DDT has had a devastating effect on the bald eagle population. Most uses of the chemical were banned in 1972, allowing for a partial recovery of the species.*

DDT caused other problems as well. Even those eggs that were not crushed sometimes did not hatch. Some of the eaglets that did hatch died from eating poisoned food; eventually so did their parents.

Ultimately, adults were simply unable to reproduce at all. The bald eagle population began falling quickly. Activists began to protest the use of DDT. For example, Rachel Carson pointed out the dangers of the pesticide in her famous book, *Silent Spring,* in 1962.

The government had to act quickly before bald eagles became extinct in the United States. By 1967, the number of surviving eagles in the United States was so low, the bald eagle was added to the Endangered Species List.[3]

Federal government officials were shocked when they realized the devastating effects that DDT had on the bald eagle as well as other birds and mammals. The United States government banned most uses of the chemical in 1972.

Since then, the bald eagle population has steadily increased. They are no longer listed as endangered. In 1995, the U.S. Fish and Wildlife Service downgraded the bald eagle from endangered to threatened. Threatened means that a species is in danger of becoming endangered. Bald eagles will have continued protection under the law.

The Endangered Species Act of 1973 protects both bald and golden eagles. Over the years, the government passed laws that made it illegal to possess dead or live eagles, kill them, harass them, or take their feathers or eggs. Other laws that protect bald eagles are the Migratory Bird Treaty Act of 1918 and the Lacey Act of 1981. According to the U.S. Fish and Wildlife Service, the eagles are the only bird or mammal to have their own law, the Bald Eagle and Golden Eagle Protection Act of 1940.

Chapter 4 ▶

America's National Symbol

The irony in the United States' poor treatment of these large raptors is that the bald eagle has long been America's majestic symbol of freedom. On July 4, 1776, Benjamin Franklin, John Adams, and Thomas Jefferson were given the job of creating the seal for the new government of the United States of America. Most of America's founding fathers felt the bald eagle was a living symbol of freedom,

Challenger - Microsoft Internet Explorer

File   Edit   View   Favorites   Tools   Help

Address http://www.eagles.org/challenger.html   Go

Done   Internet

▲ On June 20, 1782, the bald eagle became the national symbol of the United States. Shown above is Challenger, a bald eagle who has greatly increased public awareness of the plight of the species.

spirit, and integrity. However, Benjamin Franklin did not. He felt the bald eagle had a bad moral character and was lazy, because it stole food from other birds. He also felt the bald eagle was a coward, because a small bird, called the kingbird, attacks the bald eagle and chases it from its area. Franklin wanted the wild turkey as our symbol; he felt it was a more respectable bird.[1]

Despite Franklin's objections, six years later, the Second Continental Congress accepted the Great Seal of the United States with the bald eagle, not the turkey. In the center of the Great Seal is an eagle holding a shield. There are thirteen red and white stripes on the shield. The stripes represent the first thirteen states. The bald eagle's right claw holds an olive branch, containing thirteen olives and leaves. The left claw holds thirteen arrows. The olive branch and arrows stand for "the power of peace and war." In its beak, the bald eagle holds a scroll. There are thirteen letters in the motto, "*E Pluribus Unum*." This means, "Out of Many, One."

Later, President Theodore Roosevelt chose the bald eagle as the national emblem. The president felt the bald eagle represented power.[2]

President Truman changed the direction of the eagle to fact its right talon on the Seal of the President of the United States on October 25, 1945. The bald eagle had faced its left talon that clutches the arrows, signifying war. Now, the eagle faces the right talon, which holds the olive branch, representing peace.

▶ Famous Bald Eagles

One of the most famous bald eagles in American history was "Old Abe." He was the mascot of the Eighth Regiment of Wisconsin during the Civil War. He accompanied

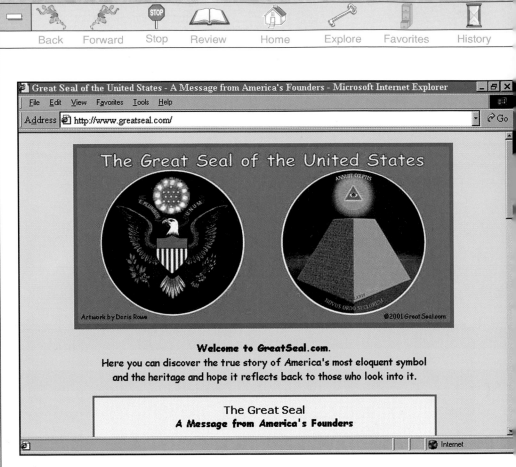

▲ The bald eagle can be found on the national seal (shown above) and the presidential seal, as well as the back of American gold coins, the silver dollar, the half dollar, and the quarter.

soldiers in no fewer than twenty battles and thirty skirmishes. Old Abe was very lucky in battle; not one drop of his blood was ever spilled.[3]

Another famous bald eagle is named Challenger. He was rescued as an eaglet during a storm. Today, he travels the country, educating people about conservation and ways to help the bald eagle. Challenger has been trained to fly over major-league baseball stadiums when the National Anthem is sung. He performed at the Olympics in Atlanta in 1996. In addition, he has been an invited guest at the White House.

▶ Government Permits

For some people, the eagle, and even eagle parts, are a sacred part of religious ceremonies. Eagle feathers and other body parts may only be used for certain purposes. The United States and Canadian governments issue special permits for the use of eagle parts. The feathers may be used for scientific research, exhibition, and American Indian religious and cultural events.

In the early 1970s, the U.S. Fish and Wildlife Service created the National Eagle Repository. This facility provides American Indians with golden eagle or bald eagle

▲ *America's founding fathers felt that the majestic bald eagle best exemplified the spirit of liberty that created the United States.*

▲ *Eagle feathers are sometimes used in religious and cultural events.*

feathers for religious purposes. By giving feathers to tribes, the pressure to take birds from the wild is reduced. The bald eagle population is thereby protected. Eagle parts are to be handed down from one tribal generation to the next. The parts may never be sold, bought, or traded. American Indians may not give feathers or other eagle parts to anyone outside their tribes.

Survival and Recovery

Since the 1960s, the bald eagle population has grown to 6,051 nesting pairs in 2002.[1] This total includes all states, except Hawaii and Alaska. There are also an unknown number of single eagles. The count is obtained by data collected from government agencies and tribes.

🔺 Bald eagles can be found in many national parks all over the country, including Grand Teton National Park in Wyoming.

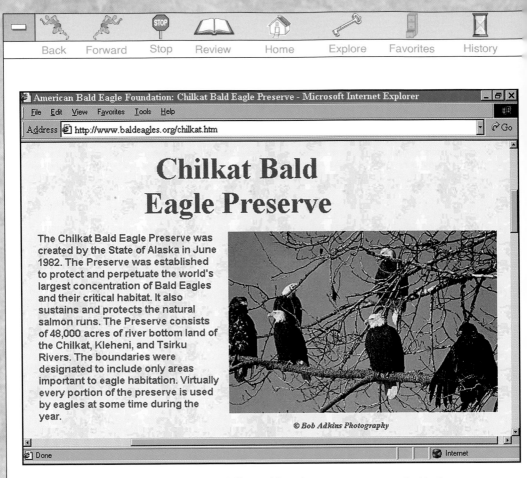

Chilkat Bald Eagle Preserve

The Chilkat Bald Eagle Preserve was created by the State of Alaska in June 1982. The Preserve was established to protect and perpetuate the world's largest concentration of Bald Eagles and their critical habitat. It also sustains and protects the natural salmon runs. The Preserve consists of 48,000 acres of river bottom land of the Chilkat, Kleheni, and Tsirku Rivers. The boundaries were designated to include only areas important to eagle habitation. Virtually every portion of the preserve is used by eagles at some time during the year.

© Bob Adkins Photography

Located in Alaska, the Chilkat Bald Eagle Preserve was created in June 1982 to protect the bald eagle. This 48,000-acre preserve is home to the largest concentration of bald eagles in the world.

Remaining Threats

The U.S. Fish and Wildlife Service has listed two main dangers that continue to threaten bald eagles. One is habitat loss. This will continue to be a problem as people move into undeveloped areas. The other major threat is still water pollution.

Other threats that can cause injury or death to bald eagles are illegal shooting, lead shot, traps set for other animals, poisons, collisions with vehicles and trains, and starvation. Additional concerns that threaten the safety of bald eagles are windmills, power lines, and disease. Power lines are particularly problematic. Eagles like to perch on them, and then swoop down to attack their prey. Unfortunately, their wingspan is likely to touch the wires, and that is usually fatal.

Because of government and public awareness, some threats to bald eagles have been greatly reduced. Dangers from some pesticides are less. Many bald eagles have died from lead poisoning by eating birds shot with lead shotgun shells, as well as fish and birds poisoned by lead shot in the water. When the use of lead shot was outlawed for hunting, another threat to the bald eagles was reduced but has not disappeared. Lead shot is still present in the mud of lakes and ponds where hunters have shot at ducks and geese in the past. These birds that eagles eat for food still sometimes feed in the contaminated mud, ingesting old lead shot.

Some companies are spending extra money to bury power lines. They are also building safer nesting platforms on transmissions towers.[2] These are steps in the right direction to provide eagles with safe places to live and perch.

▶ Recovery

Recovery is the process of increasing the species' population to the point where it is no longer threatened with extinction. This method allows the species to survive long-term. The U.S. Fish and Wildlife Service began a recovery program for the bald eagle. They opened the Patuxent Wildlife Research Center near Laurel, Maryland. The purpose of this facility was to breed bald eagles in captivity. When healthy eaglets were old enough, they would be released into the wild.

At the center, the bald eagle's first clutch of eggs are removed so they can not be tampered with. Scientists artificially incubate the eggs until they hatch. Usually, the female lays a second clutch. The parents are then allowed to incubate the second set of egg.

The Patuxent Wildlife Research Center was highly successful. It ended its program in 1988, because the bald eagle began to reproduce well enough in the wild. The program produced 124 bald eagles. These eagles were used to restock wild populations in several areas of the country.

Stronger enforcement of laws has further helped bald eagle recovery. Conservation agencies bought millions of acres of land to protect bald eagle habitats. In addition, hundreds of bald eagles have been placed in previously unoccupied but suitable, habitats.

▶ Reintroduction

Universities, private organizations, and state governments use two methods of reintroduction. One is called the captive-hatched program. When two or more eggs are laid, one egg is removed from the nest. This egg is placed in another bald eagle's nest. The new foster parents may not have been able to reproduce, or their own eggs did not hatch. Foster parents will incubate the egg and raise the eaglet as their own.[3]

Hacking is another method used in the reintroduction program. The eggs are removed from their nests and incubated by humans. After the eggs hatch, humans feed the eaglets while avoiding any direct contact with them. When the chicks are eight weeks old, they are moved to a man-made nest enclosed by bars in a high tower. This is called a hacking tower. The towers are often inside a bird sanctuary.

The bald eagle was added to the Endangered Species List in 1967. The U.S. Fish and Wildlife Service has recommended delisting the bird due to the successful reduction of its main threats.

A sanctuary is a government-protected area that is safe for the birds. At around twelve weeks of age, the bars are removed from around the nest. Until they can hunt for themselves, humans continue to feed the eaglets. Scientists hope the artificially-raised bald eagles will remain in the area, and breed and nest as adults.

Since the bald eagle was added to the Endangered Species List in 1967, the federal government has spent approximately one million dollars per year on eagle recovery. Money is also spent on enforcing bald eagle protection laws and aggressively prosecuting those who break these laws.

▶ Removal From the Endangered Species List

The U.S. Fish and Wildlife Service has recommended delisting (removing) the bald eagle from the Endangered Species List.[4] The government is considering delisting, because the main threats to the bald eagle have been reduced. Healthy eaglets are being born in the wild, and the population is steadily increasing.

Presently, the federal government is working closely with the states on recovery issues. Most of the states have agreed to a five-year plan to monitor the bald eagle. If the bald eagle population begins to decline during this five-year period, the U.S. Fish and Wildlife Services could place the bald eagle back on the Endangered Species List.[5]

If the bald eagle is delisted, the Migratory Bird Treaty Act, the Bald Eagle Protection Act, and other laws will still protect the species. Recovery involves federal and state government cooperation, conservation programs, and federal and state laws against bald eagle hunting. Educating the public is also important.

▶ How You Can Help

As a private citizen, you can help the bald eagle in many ways. If you see a dead or injured animal on the road, call your city or town's game commission or streets department. They will remove the carrion. This will reduce vehicle and bald eagle collisions. If you find a dead or injured bald eagle, you should call the state wildlife agency or the U.S. Fish and Wildlife Service. You can also join a local bird-watching group to learn more about bald eagles.

▲ *Cooperation of state and federal governments as well as conservation programs and public education are necessary to ensure the continued existence of the bald eagle.*

Your school or classroom can adopt a bald eagle or a nest, take part in the American Eagle Day Letter Campaign, or become involved with a bird of prey education show.

▶ Success

According to the U.S. Fish and Wildlife Service, the banning of DDT and passage of the Endangered Species Act are the two main reasons for the recovery of the bald eagle.

The recovery of the bald eagle is not complete. However, many believe the repopulation of America's national bird is truly a success story.

This series is based on the Endangered and Threatened Wildlife list compiled by the U.S. Fish and Wildlife Service (USFWS). Each book explores an endangered or threatened animal, tells why it has become endangered or threatened, and explains the efforts being made to restore the species' population.

The United States Fish and Wildlife Service, in the Department of the Interior, and the National Marine Fisheries Service, in the Department of Commerce, share responsibility for administration of the Endangered Species Act.

In 1973, Congress took the farsighted step of creating the Endangered Species Act, widely regarded as the world's strongest and most effective wildlife conservation law. It set an ambitious goal: to reverse the alarming trend of human-caused extinction that threatened the ecosystems we all share.

The complete list of Endangered and Threatened Wildlife and Plants can be found at
http://endangered.fws.gov/wildlife.html#Species

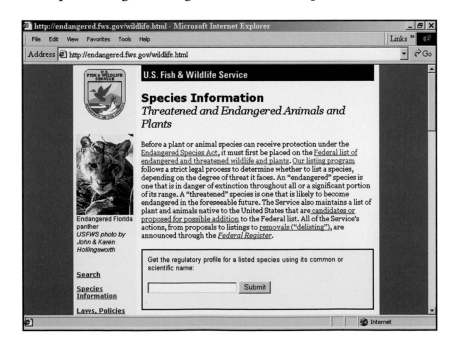

Chapter Notes

Chapter 1. The Bald Eagle

1. "History of the Bald Eagle," *American Bald Eagle Information*, p. 2, 1996–2001, <http://www.baldeagleinfo.com/eagle/eagle11.html> (December 31, 2001).

2. "American Bald Eagle," *Bald Eagle*, p. 2, n.d., <http://www.usflag.org/bald.eagle.html> (January 13, 2002).

Chapter 2. Profile of a Bald Eagle

1. "American Bald Eagle," *Bald Eagle*, p. 1, n.d., <http://www.usflag.org/bald.eagle.html> (January 13, 2002).

2. "American Bald Eagle Description," p. 1, 1996–2001, <http://www.baldeagleinfo.com/eagle/eagle8.html> (January 4, 2002).

3. "Bald Eagle," *UAMZ: Feature Creatures*, p. 1, 2001, <http://www.biology.ualberta.ca/uamz.hp/eagle.html> (December 26, 2002).

4. "Voice," *American Bald Eagle Information*, p. 2, 1996–2001, <http://www.baldeagleinfo.com/eagle/eagle8.html> (January 4, 2002).

5. "Diet and Feeding Habits," *American Bald Eagle Information*, p. 1, 1996–2001, <http://www.baldeagleinfo.com/eagle/eagle3.html> (January 4, 2002).

Chapter 3. A Threatened Species

1. Charles L. Cadieux, *These Are The Endangered* (Washington, D.C.: Stone Wall Press, Inc., 1981), p. 132.

2. David W. Daum, "Eagles," *ADF&G's Wildlife Notebook Series*, p. 2, 1994, <http://www.state.ak.us/adfg/notebook/bird/eagles.htm> (January 7, 2002).

3. "Bald Eagle," *Texas Parks and Wildlife, Threatened and Endangered Species*, p. 1, n.d., <http://www.tpwd.state.tx.us/nature/endang/birds/baldeagl.htm> (February 5, 2002).

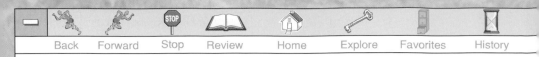
Chapter 4. America's National Symbol

1. Eagle Facts, "History," p. 1, n.d., <http://library.thinkquest.org/Joo2383/history.htm> (January 13, 2002).

2. The Eagle Watch, "More About Eagles," p. 3, n.d., <http://www.eaglewatch.com/moreabouteagles.htm> (January 21, 2002).

3. "Old Abe," *American Bald Eagle Information*, p. 1, 1996–2001, <http://www.baldeagleinfo.com/eagle/oldabe.html> (March 8, 2002).

Chapter 5. Survival and Recovery

1. Personal e-mail from Cindy Hoffman, Public Affairs Specialist, U.S. Fish and Wildlife Service, Washington, D.C., (April 15, 2002).

2. "Bald Eagle Recovery," *American Bald Eagle Information*, p. 1, 1996–2001, <http://www.baldeagleinfo.com/eagle/future.html> (May 27, 2002).

3. Ibid., p. 2.

4. U.S. Fish & Wildlife Service, 'Bald Eagle Recovery: Question and Answers,' Question 15, n.d., <http://midwest.fws.gov/eagle/success/bequanda.pdf> (April 26, 2002).

5. U.S. Fish & Wildlife Service, *Endangered Species Fact Sheet*, "Bald Eagle: Monitoring if Delisted," p. 1, n.d., <http://midwest.fws.gov/eagle/protect/Bemonitr.pdf> (April 26, 2002).

Further Reading

Barghusen, John D. *The Bald Eagle*. Farmington Hills, Mich.: Gale Group, 1998.

Collard, Sneed B. III. *Birds of Prey: A Look at Daytime Raptors*. New York: Grolier Publication, 1999.

Dennis, Roy. *Golden Eagles*. Stillwater, Minn.: Colin Baxter Photography, 1997.

Evert, Laura. *Eagles*. Minnetonka, Minn.: North Word Press, 2001.

Grambo, Rebecca L. *Eagles*. Stillwater, Minn.: Voyageur Press, Inc., 1999.

Hutchinson, Alan. *Just Eagle: A Wildlife Watcher's Guides*. Minocqua, Wisc.: Willow Creek Press, 2000.

Jones, Jemima Parry. *The Eagle & Birds of Prey*. New York: Dorling Kindersley Publishing, Inc., 2000.

Patent, Dorothy Hinshaw. *The Bald Eagle Returns*. New York: Houghton Mifflin Company, 2000.

Peck, George K. *Hawks and Eagles*. North Mankato, Minn.: Smart Apple Media, 1997.

Richardson, Adele. *Eagles*. Mankato, Minn.: The Creative Company, 1995.

Rue, Leonard Lee Rue, III. *Birds of Prey: A Portrait of the Animal World*. New York: Todtri Productions, Ltd., 1998.

Savage, Candace. *Eagles of North America*. Vancouver B.C.: Douglas and McIntyr, Ltd., 2000.

Scholz, Floyd. *Birds of Prey*. Mechanicsburg, Penn.: Stackpole Books, 1993.

Wyss, Hal H. *Eagles: A Portrait Of The Animal World*. New York: Todtri Book Publishers, Ltd., 1998.